HOCKEY
THE PLAYERS

DAVID AND PATRICIA ARMENTROUT

The Rourke Press, Inc.
Vero Beach, Florida 32964

Patricia and David Armentrout specialize in nonfiction writing and have had several book series published for primary schools. They reside in Cincinnati with their two children.

PROJECT EDITORS:
Dick Doughty is a former Elementary School teacher who now operates his own business. He coached hockey for 9 years from the minor level through Junior "A." Dick is a certified Level 3 OMHA referee and is currently Referee-in-Chief for his hometown minor hockey association.

Rob Purdy has been a Secondary School teacher for 16 years. He is a certified Advance I hockey coach and a NCCP coaching instructor. Rob has coached hockey for 10 years in the OMHA, with a Pee Wee championship in 1997.

PHOTO CREDITS:
All photos © Kim Karpeles except © Rick Stewart/Allsport: page 11; © Todd Warshaw/Allsport: page 19; © Craig Melvin/Allsport: page 34; © East Coast Studios page 4

EDITORIAL SERVICES:
Penworthy Learning Systems

Library of Congress Cataloging-in-Publication Data

Armentrout, David, 1962-
   Hockey—the players / David Armentrout, Patricia Armentrout.
     p. cm. — (Hockey)
   Includes index.
   Summary: Describes the various playing positions in hockey, their responsibilities, and how they work together as a team.
   ISBN 1-57103-223-1
   1. Hockey—Juvenile literature. [1. Hockey.] I. Armentrout, Patricia, 1960-
II. Title. III. Series: Armentrout, David, 1962- Hockey.
QV847.25.A757 1998
796.962—dc21   98–28404
                                                CIP
                                                 AC

Printed in the USA

TABLE OF CONTENTS

PLAYERS' POSITIONS

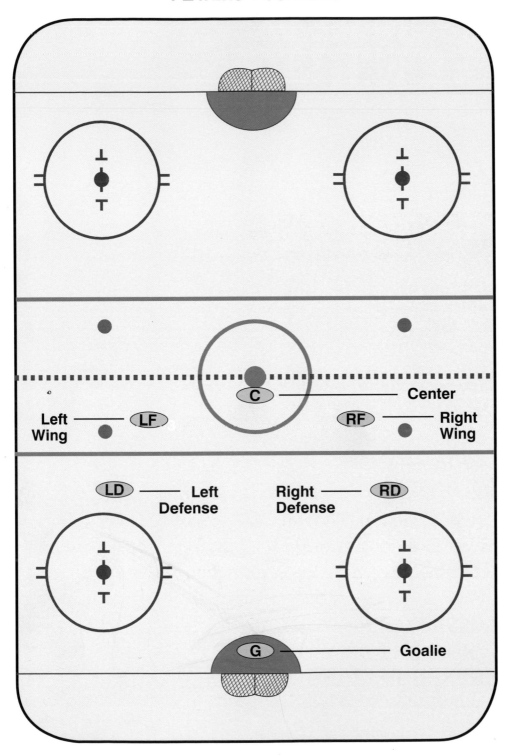

There are six players on the ice during a game.

THE CENTER

A hockey team can have no more than six players on the ice at any one time. A team's lineup consists of three forward positions, two defense positions, and a goalie. Sometimes, though, a coach may change this lineup.

Most hockey players specialize at one position. A player who learns and practices the skills of all the positions will be a better team player. As a newcomer to the sport, make sure you experience each position. After all, how will you know what position you enjoy most unless you give them all a try?

The two types of forward position are center and wings. The center directs the team's play at both ends of the rink, much like a football team's quarterback who directs his team on the field. The center works with the left and right wing and leads the team's attack.

Often one of the best players on the team, the center, requires varied skills. A center should be a master at the face-off, a first-rate passer, and able to shoot as well as any player on the team. Of course, the center must also be a top-notch skater to lead his or her team in both the **attack zone** and **defensive zone**.

The center skates up and down the middle of the ice, passing the puck back and forth between the wings. The center starts at center ice, but he or she often chases the puck wherever it goes. All three forwards (left wing, center, and right wing) play offensively, getting the puck to the net and setting up shots on goal. Defensively, the center tries to keep the puck in the attack zone, and does this by harassing the opponent's puck carrier.

★ **COACH'S CORNER**

A center usually takes a face-off. When you practice face-offs, focus on the puck in the official's hand.

The forward line is in position for a face-off.

All players wear protective clothing and a helmet with a face mask.

Some centers are fast and powerful skaters. Some dominate the opposing players with their size. Other centers are playmakers. They concentrate their efforts on setting up the wings to score. Some centers combine good attack skills, scoring abilities, and tough defensive moves.

Most teams have three or four center players who dress to play a game. The first-line center is usually a playmaker or a good scorer. The second-line center may also have good offensive skills and be a major scorer for the team. Coaches place centers with strong defense abilities on the third line. When a third-line center starts a period, the main job is to keep the opponent from scoring, by checking the other team's first-line center.

COACH'S CORNER

Goal protection should be your first concern when taking a face-off in your defensive zone. If you win the face-off, you should immediately break out of your zone and start your attack.

Famous Centers

The player at center is often the best-known member of a team. The center often controls the puck, scores many of the goals, and takes most of the face-offs in a game. If you are a good center, you definitely will be noticed by hockey fans. However, this by no means diminishes the importance of the other positions on the team.

For example, what hockey fan doesn't know Wayne Gretzky? Many fans and teammates consider Gretzky to be the greatest to ever play the game. In fact he is called the "Great One," a nickname given to him at an early age.

All would agree that Canadian-born Gretzky is a superb center. He is known for quick thinking and split-second reactions, not fast skating. Gretzky is a playmaker who works with the "wingers" to score goals.

Forwards pass the puck back and forth as they skate up the ice.

"The Great One" Wayne Gretzky.

Wayne Gretzky holds more National Hockey League (NHL) records than any other player. He is the all-time leading scorer and the all-time leader in assists. At the end of the 1997 season, Gretzky had won the Hart Memorial Trophy (MVP—most valuable player in a regular season) nine times.

Mario Lemieux—another great center from Canada—is also a famous hockey player. Lemieux was drafted into the NHL in 1985 and started playing for the Pittsburgh Penguins. Just three years later he won his first of three MVP awards. Though missing an entire season of play due to back problems and a bout with Hodgkin's Disease, Mario Lemieux led the Penguins to the conference finals in 1996. He played hockey for the Penguins until his retirement in 1997.

Mario Lemieux is known for the way he controlled the pace of the game with his shooting and passing skills. He won the Art Ross Trophy (the most points in a season) five times and helped his team win the Stanley Cup Championship twice.

CHAPTER TWO

THE WINGS

The forward line is made up of the center and two wings, or "wingers." The wings are designated by the side of the rink they are responsible for—the right wing and the left wing. A wing's main job is to score goals. Wingers move up and down the ice in the direction of the play. In other words, wingers go where the puck goes and are often on the offense.

Wingers work with the center, passing the puck and setting up shots on goal. All forwards need to have strong passing and shooting skills as well as strong skating skills.

The wings work close to the boards while the center usually plays the middle. Generally a left wing covers the left side of the ice, and a right wing covers the right side of the ice. Often, though, wings find themselves on opposite sides of the rink. Sometimes wingers will cross paths and end up trading sides. This move is meant to confuse the other team's defensemen, leaving one or both wings open to opportunity.

In the past, a right-handed shot (player who shoots with right hand) played right wing; a left-handed shot, the left wing. Today's wingers shoot just as well with either hand. In fact, they have a wide range of skills that includes "shooting off the pass." In this kind of shot, a player receives a pass and takes a shot immediately, not wasting time by stopping the puck and setting it up for a shot. Shooting off the pass is also called a "one-timer." A wing who can take one-time shots greatly increases opportunities to score goals.

★ DID YOU KNOW?

Forwards weave, or cut across each other's path, in the neutral zone. Weaving makes it easier to pass and receive the puck.

The team who gains control of the puck will be on the offense.

A coach will send in plays with a line change.

Hockey is physically demanding with non stop action. Coaches usually make a **substitution** on the fly (without stopping play) to keep a player from becoming too tired. Typically, a wing is on the ice for 30 to 45 seconds before being replaced. This constant rotation helps to keep players fresh and playing at their peak.

Even with frequent substitutions, players must be fit. Wingers move up and down the ice throughout a game and can't afford to get winded. They need to spend a lot of practice time just skating to increase their **endurance**. Wings sometimes take face-offs and should spend plenty of time practicing them, too.

All wingers must be as good defensively as they are offensively. Forwards need to spend a lot of time on **forechecking** skills. Forechecking is attacking and covering the opponent. The instant a team loses possession of the puck, one or more forwards should go into action, aggressively forechecking the opponent and keeping them in their own defensive zone.

★ **DID YOU KNOW?**

A sharp wing will reach ahead to receive a "bad" pass with only one hand on the stick. If a pass comes too close to a winger's feet, he or she kicks it out toward the blade of the stick.

Famous Wingers

One of the toughest players in the history of the NHL is Gordie Howe. A brilliant winger, Howe is known as "Mr. Hockey" to fans and players alike. Gordie Howe joined the NHL in 1946. In 1973, at age 45, he moved to the World Hockey Association (WHA) league and began playing with the Houston Aeros. That same season he won the league MVP award. When the WHA folded in 1979, Howe rejoined the NHL. He retired, at age 51, the next year.

Players struggle for control of the puck.

Jaromir Jagr of the Pittsburg Penguins.

During his career, Gordie Howe collected 1675 penalty minutes, earning his tough guy reputation. More importantly, Howe scored 1846 points in 26 seasons with the NHL and won the league MVP award six times. The nickname "Mr. Hockey" was well earned.

Jaromir Jagr is a right winger playing for the Pittsburgh Penguins. A powerful and dedicated forward, Jagr started skating at age 3. He is from Kladno in the Czech Republic (formerly Czechoslovakia), and loves to travel back home during the off-season. Jagr played in a Junior Hockey league as a boy and was drafted by the NHL when he was 18. As much as he enjoys the serious game of hockey, Jagr enjoys playing jokes on his teammates and has a reputation for being the team comedian.

CHAPTER THREE

THE DEFENSEMEN

The defensemen's main responsibility is to defend their team's goal, but there is much more to the job. Defensemen also play an offensive role. Defensemen should be willing and able to lead a **breakout** into the attack zone. Some defensemen even score goals regularly. A well-rounded team that has players capable of playing offense as easily as defense is sure to win its share of games.

The left defenseman usually covers the left side of the rink and the right defenseman covers the right side; however, defensemen may cross over to the other side of the rink to maintain their **strategic** play. Defensemen, nicknamed "blueliners," try to keep the opposing team from crossing into their defensive zone (over their blue line).

Defensemen must be strong and aggressive, not afraid to body-check now and then—to keep an opponent from becoming too confident.

Defensemen should keep the **slot** covered at all times. When the puck, and, therefore, the action is on the defender's right side, the left defenseman should cover the slot. If the action moves to the left side, the right defenseman should cover the slot. Of course, there are always exceptions to the rule. A team that plays well together reads their teammates' movements and "covers" when one member moves out of his or her normal area.

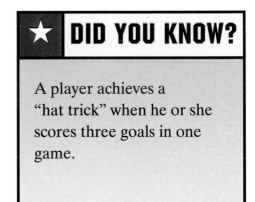

★ **DID YOU KNOW?**

A player achieves a "hat trick" when he or she scores three goals in one game.

Wingers skate parallel up the ice.

It is important to keep your stick out in front to receive a pass.

Defensemen are really a team's third line of defense. Forechecking and **back-checking** by the forwards are the first and second line. If an opponent breaks out into your defensive zone, it is up to your defensemen and the goalie (the last line of defense) to regain possession of the puck.

Defense Strategy

Coaches have many defense strategies. One common strategy works like this: As the opposing team attacks, their defensemen come in as far as the **point** positions (just inside the blue line and close to the boards). Your team's two wingers cover them. Two of the opponent's forwards try to get into position to score as the third carries the puck. Your strong-side defenseman (the defenseman on the same side as the puck carrier) covers the puck carrier while the weak side defenseman covers the slot close to the goal crease, and an opposing forward trying to get into scoring position. Your third forward, the center, covers their third forward.

★ DID YOU KNOW?

A player in possession of the puck might "fake out" the opponents by moving the puck or his or her body in one direction and then quickly in the opposite direction. Faking out an opponent is called a "deke."

Coaches have their players practice defense strategies over and over. Drills help defensemen work on their skating, stick-checking, and body-checking skills. A good defenseman uses these skills to keep an opponent away from the goal and to fight for control of the puck along the boards. Once a defenseman gains control of the puck he or she must use offensive skills. Defense players need to be able to move the puck up the ice and pass it to a forward, who takes it back into the attack zone.

All strategies require practice. Youth teams generally practice one to two times a week.

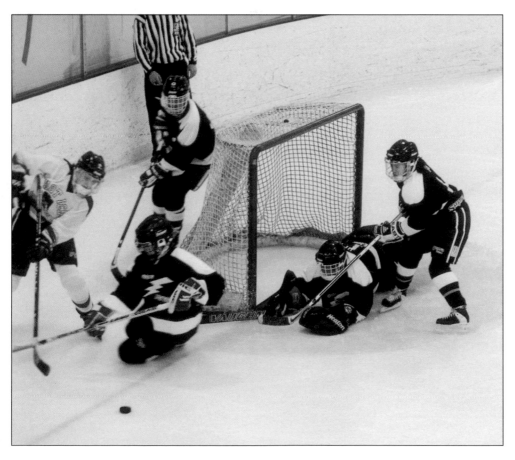

Non-stop action close to the goal.

An illegal check using the knee.

Famous Defensemen

Defenseman Bobby Orr began his first season with the NHL in 1966. He won the Calder Trophy for Rookie of the Year. The next eight seasons Orr won the Norris Trophy for best defensemen. What made Bobby Orr great? Orr started skating at age four, and by the time he started playing Canadian squirt hockey in kindergarten he had already learned some good passing and puck control skills. In the NHL, Bobby Orr is known as the man who changed the way hockey is played. He played tough like a defenseman while skating with speed and grace.

Although he ended his career playing for the Chicago Blackhawks, he is best known for his success while with the Boston Bruins. It was Bobby Orr who led the Bruins to their first Stanley Cup in 29 years. Despite his bad knees, Bobby Orr skated with extreme power and managed to score plenty of goals, too.

CHAPTER FOUR

THE GOALIE

Anyone who has ever watched an ice hockey game has certainly noticed the masked player crouching in front of the goal. Goalies may look a little odd dressed from head to toe in protective gear, but they're dressed that way for good reason. Goalies put themselves in the path of a hard rubber puck that can reach speeds of over 100 miles an hour.

Almost every piece of goalie equipment is made to take the rough treatment that goalkeepers must bear. Before you consider playing goal, make sure you have the proper equipment and that you are wearing it correctly. It's simply a matter of safety.

Goalkeepers wear goalie skates, legpads, kneepads, a protective cup or pelvic protector, padded pants, and chest protection. A goalie also wears a helmet with a full face mask and a throat/neck protector. A goalie's stick has an extra-wide blade to help stop the puck.

A goalie wears two different gloves. One glove, called the blocker, is worn on the stick hand. The blocker is a flat rectangular pad on the back of a glove. It blocks, or deflects (turns away), the puck. The goalie wears a catcher's glove on the other hand. This glove is used to catch fast-moving pucks before they enter the net.

A goalie's stance, or body position, is key. A proper stance allows a full range of motion.

For the proper stance, keep your legs close together (but not touching) with your weight on the balls of your feet. Your stick blade should rest flat on the ice. The middle of the blade should line up roughly with your chin. If your stick is positioned properly your blocker pad will also be in the right position—to your side and lined up with the top of your legpads. Your catcher's glove should be open and ready for action. From this balanced stance, you can carry out nearly any defensive move.

★ **DID YOU KNOW?**

A goalie is the only player on a team who is allowed to close his or her hand around the puck. A teammate may bat the puck to another teammate in the defending zone; but if anyone but the goalie closes his or her hand around the puck, play is stopped and a face-off follows.

A goalie gets instruction on how to skate backwards.

Goalies use a catcher's glove to stop fast-moving pucks.

Goalie Skills

If the puck makes its way close to the goal, the goalkeeper must act quickly to gain control of it. A goalie has several options when the puck gets close. The option you choose will depend on the positions of your teammates and opponents.

If an opponent is "too close for comfort," you, as a goalkeeper, can knock the puck away with your stick; fall on the puck, freezing it and forcing a face-off; or pick it up. If you choose to pick up the puck, you can then drop it within reach of your defensemen, or drop it and use your stick to pass it to a teammate. If you choose to pick up the puck, make sure you react fast. If you don't the referee may assess a minor penalty for stopping play.

A goalie should learn many different techniques and develop a range of skills. Some skills come almost naturally, others from trial and error. Many have to be learned and practiced again and again. A goalie coach can share much of the knowledge that would take you years to pick up on your own. A coach can also spot your strong points (and make them stronger) and weak points (and help you over-come them).

DID YOU KNOW?

A puck shot "between the pipes" is a goal! A "save" is a shot that could have gone into the net but was blocked by the goalie. A game in which one team does not score is called a "shutout."

Playing goal calls for full use of a goalie's ability—body and mind. A goalie is under constant pressure to keep opponents from scoring. Some goalies feel personally responsible when they allow a goal; but hockey is a team sport, and every player is equally responsible for wins and losses. If a goalie's teammates do a good job, they will keep the puck away from the net as much as possible. A team wins together and loses together.

Dominik Hasek makes a save.

A typical goalie stance for defending goal.

Famous Goalies

One of the best goalies is Dominik Hasek, the first goalie to win the NHL's MVP award. Nicknamed "the Dominator," Hasek's hardworking, never-quit attitude puts him at the top of many fans' all-time greatest goalies list.

Standing 5 feet 11 inches (about 180 centimeters) and weighing 168 pounds (about 76 kilograms), Dominik Hasek is certainly not one of the largest goalies; but he manages to stop opponents' shots with his speed and technique. His success as a goalie with the Buffalo Sabres led him to the 1998 Winter Olympics where he defended goal for his home country the Czech Republic. It should not come as a surprise that the Czech team won the gold medal.

CHAPTER FIVE

THE COACH

The coach is a team's leader on and off the ice. A coach puts a team together and gets credit for its success or failure. Many hockey coaches are former players who want to stay involved in the game. Most of the coaches in youth leagues are volunteers, meaning they coach because they want to, not for pay. Being a volunteer coach can be stressful and time-consuming, but it can also be fun and rewarding.

A coach is a teacher. He or she helps players learn new skills. To teach, a coach has to go on the ice with the team during practice. It is essential that a coach can skate. Coaches should own the basic equipment (skates, stick, and protective gear) so that they can participate fully in the practice.

At first, a coach tries to determine the strengths and weaknesses of each player. Only then does a coach assign players to positions. Assigning players is not an easy task, and each player must accept the coach's judgment. Team sports are all about teamwork and **sportsmanship**. If a player learns these two fundamental values, then the coach has done his or her job well.

Practice Sessions

Since ice hockey is usually played on indoor rinks and few rinks are available, practice sessions are also limited—usually no longer than an hour. Most coaches follow a practice schedule to get the most out of each session.

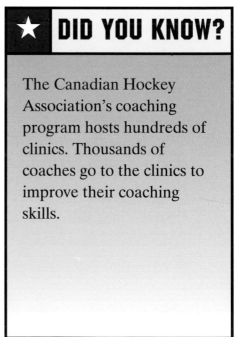

★ **DID YOU KNOW?**

The Canadian Hockey Association's coaching program hosts hundreds of clinics. Thousands of coaches go to the clinics to improve their coaching skills.

A coach shows a goalie the proper glove position.

Players receive plays from the player's bench.

A typical practice for a youth, collegiate, or professional team begins with stretching and **calisthenics**, followed by skating, passing, and shooting drills. Next a coach sets up a practice game. Most youth league teams practice two times a week, professional teams practice daily.

Some older league teams are fortunate enough to have a head coach as well as one or more assistant coaches. The head coach has final say and control of the team. An assistant coach usually is responsible for a specific area of team development, such as an offensive play coach, defensive play coach, and a goaltending coach.

Game Time

A coach is often called upon to make tough decisions. An example: Which players will be starters and which will play on the second or third line? In some advanced leagues, a coach may even have to decide whether some players will even make the team. At the lower levels, though, most coaches make sure that all players, regardless of skill level, get playing time in every game.

★ COACH'S CORNER

The home team coach has an advantage because he or she can change players last before a face-off. The visiting team can't change until play has resumed.

Coaches are not allowed on the ice during a game. They direct their teams by substituting players, sending in plays with line changes, and instructing individual players from the players' bench. The coach is there to teach and help players improve their hockey skills between games. The coach is the one person who sees the "big picture." He or she plans a team's strategy and gives advice for working together. Therefore, players should listen to their coach and show respect and appreciation.

Players review plays at a practice session.

A coach is a teacher and a team leader.

Coaching College and Pro Teams

Coaches of college and professional teams are professionals (paid to coach) themselves. Coaching is their full-time job, and coaches must be highly trained and motivated to be successful. A professional hockey coach can be compared to the president of a large company. The coach must be able to search for, hire, train, and motivate assistants and players with different backgrounds.

A coach has a thankless job if the team does not perform well. Fans and team owners quickly lose trust in a coach if the team's record is not good. On the other hand, a coach with a winning record is often looked upon as a hero. Winning coaches also earn winning salaries that make the hard work and heavy pressure easier to take.

GLOSSARY

attack zone (eh TAK ZON) — area on the ice between an opponent's blue line and goal line

back-checking (BAK CHEK ing) — covering an opponent in your own defensive zone

breakout (BRAYK OUT) — play used by an attacking team to move the puck out of the defensive zone toward the opponent's goal

calisthenics (KAL is THEN iks) — body exercises that may include small, light hand weights, but no other equipment

defensive zone (di FEN siv ZON) — area on the ice between the blue line and your team's goal line

endurance (en DOOR uns) — ability to withstand stress

forechecking (FAWR CHEK ing) — covering an opponent in your offensive zone to prevent an attack

point (POYNT) — area just inside the blue line, close to the boards, on either side of the rink

slot (SLOT) — area through the middle of the ice, between the two face-off circles, that is ideal for scoring

sportsmanship (SPORTS men ship) — playing fairly and winning and losing gracefully

GLOSSARY

strategic (streh TEE jik) — careful planning to gain an
advantage

substitutions (SUB sti TOO shunz) — players from the
players' bench taking the place of players on the ice

FURTHER READING

Find out more with these helpful books and information sites:

Davidson, John, with John Steinbreder. *Hockey for Dummies An Official Publication of the NHL.* Foster City, CA: IDG Books Worldwide, Inc., 1997.

USA Hockey. *Official Rules of Ice Hockey.* Chicago: Triumph Books, 1997.

Official Rule Book of the Canadian Hockey Association. Canadian Hockey Association, 1997.

National Hockey League, The, and others. *The Official National Hockey League 75th Anniversary Commemorative Book.* Toronto: The Canadian Publishers, 1991.

Harris, Lisa. *Hockey How to Play the All-Star Way.* Austin, TX: Raintree/Steck-Vaughn Publishers, 1994.

Canadian Hockey Association at www.canadianhockey.ca/

International Ice Hockey Federation (IIHF) at www.iihf.com

National Hockey League at www.nhl.com

USA Hockey, Inc. at www.usahockey.com

INDEX